Author:
Roger Canavan is an award-winning author of more than 60 books for young readers, covering science and other nonfiction subjects. Regular school visits and science experiments conducted with his three children keep him connected with his wide readership as well as with the latest school curriculum developments.

Series creator:
David Salariya was born in Dundee, Scotland. He has illustrated a wide range of books and has created and designed many new series for publishers in the UK and overseas. David established The Salariya Book Company in 1989. He lives in Brighton, England, with his wife, illustrator Shirley Willis, and their son, Jonathan.

Artists:
Isobel Lundie, Bryan Beach, Jared Green, Sam Bridges, and Shutterstock.

Editor:
Nick Pierce

PAPER FROM
SUSTAINABLE
FORESTS

© The Salariya Book Company Ltd MMXIX
No part of this publication may be reproduced in whole or in part, or stored in a retrieval system, or transmitted in any form or by any means, electronic, mechanical, photocopying, recording or otherwise, without written permission of the publisher. For information regarding permission, write to the copyright holder.

Published in Great Britain in 2019 by
The Salariya Book Company Ltd
25 Marlborough Place, Brighton BN1 1UB

Library of Congress Cataloging-in-Publication Data

Names: Canavan, Roger, author.
Title: The science of vehicles : the turbo-charged truth about trucks and cars / written by Roger Canavan.
Description: New York, NY : Franklin Watts, an imprint of Scholastic Inc., 2019. | Series: The science of engineering | Includes index.
Identifiers: LCCN 2018034874| ISBN 9780531131985 (library binding) | ISBN 9780531133989 (pbk.)
Subjects: LCSH: Motor vehicles--Design and construction--Juvenile literature. | Automobiles--Design and construction--Juvenile literature.
Classification: LCC TL147 .C3345 2019 | DDC 629.2--dc23

All rights reserved.
Published in 2019 in the United States
by Franklin Watts
An imprint of Scholastic Inc.

Printed and bound in China.
Printed on paper from sustainable sources.
1 2 3 4 5 6 7 8 9 10 R 28 27 26 25 24 23 22 21 20 19

The Science of Vehicles

The Turbo-Charged Truth About Trucks and Cars

written by
Roger Canavan

Franklin Watts®
An Imprint of Scholastic Inc.

Contents

Introduction

Look at any busy city street and you'll see a big collection of cars and trucks. You've probably ridden many times in some of them—passenger cars, school buses, or taxis. But sharing road space with those are delivery vans, fuel trucks, and emergency vehicles. And outside cities you'll find farm vehicles, giant construction trucks, and even cars that seem more like boats or planes. This book looks at the science that lies behind that wide range of cars and trucks. You'll see how some of the same scientific principles that you learn in the classroom—with terms like force, energy, and motion—are at work with these vehicles. Whether it's gasoline engines powered with timed explosions, electric vehicles that run on batteries, or rocket-like high-speed cars with sleek shapes, it's science that makes all of them go.

Drivers of horseless carriages in many countries had to have someone walk in front with a red flag to warn pedestrians and horses of the approaching vehicle.

Paving the Way

The breakthroughs of the Industrial Revolution meant that people could harness new types of power. And it wasn't long before engineers and inventors were testing these new technologies to find better—and faster—ways of transporting people and goods. By the end of the nineteenth century, the technology known as internal combustion had become dominant. Gasoline-powered vehicles signaled the end of the age of the horse. Engineers and inventors saw the potential and began finding new ways to produce speed and power—efforts that continue to this day.

End of an Era

Horses had provided transportation for centuries, and most people were familiar with how far a horse could ride in an hour, or how much farmland a team of horses could plow in a day. Eighteenth-century Scottish engineer James Watt invented the word "horsepower" to compare the output of steam engines with the power of draft horses—horses that pull heavy loads.

Steam Power?

ust as the Industrial Revolution was built on steam power, early designers used steam to drive their cars. The force from water heated into steam could power machinery. Soon it became clear, though, that steam engines on cars were clumsy and dangerous.

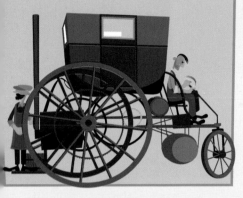

Even today's engineers measure the output of vehicles in horsepower —a throwback to the time when cars were just replacing horses for transportation.

New Type of Fuel

German inventor Karl Benz combined his love of bicycles with his knowledge of trains to produce the first real automobile in 1885. His three-wheeled "motorwagen" looks spindly to us, but its engine design paved the way for the future. Benz used a mixture of air and gasoline (a fuel that burns) to release the energy needed to move the car. This technique, called internal combustion, is still used in most cars.

Fascinating Fact

In 1769, more than a century before Benz's Motorwagen, Frenchman Nicolas-Joseph Cugnot developed a steam-powered tractor. This vehicle was heavy and hard to steer. Things got worse for Cugnot two years later when he had the world's first car accident—crashing through a brick wall in Paris and winding up in prison.

Energy Transfer

Scientists define energy as the ability to do work. You can't create or destroy energy, but you can store, release, or transfer it. The gas from a filling station has potential energy—energy that's waiting to be used in some way. The spark from the spark plug causes the gas to burn, which turns it into mechanical energy—which is needed to move the car.

A turbocharger uses the force of the exhaust to power a fanlike device that pumps even more air into the cylinder, allowing it to mix with even more fuel—giving the car more power.

Under the Hood and Beyond

Gas from the vehicle's fuel tank flows to the engine, where the rhythmic sparks from the spark plugs cause a constant series of mini-explosions. Those explosions—the reason behind the name internal combustion—provide the power.

But that's just the start of a process that has energy constantly being transferred in a car or truck. Ingenious design channels the energy so that the rear (or sometimes front) wheels keep turning—moving the car forward or backward.

Got a Light?

An electrical signal causes the spark plug in each cylinder to spark, igniting the air and fuel mixture that had been squished up inside the cylinder. By the time the piston has been pushed down again (because of this mini-explosion), then up again (getting rid of the exhaust), then down again (sucking in more air and fuel), then back up (compression)—it's ready to spark again.

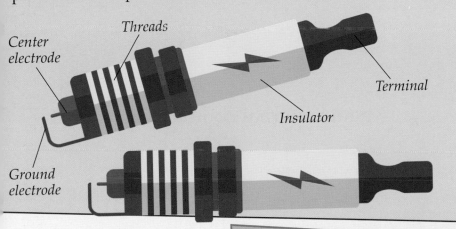

Center electrode

Threads

Terminal

Insulator

Ground electrode

Going for a Spin

Wheels

Engine

Driveshaft

Axle

Differential

The up-down motion of the pistons causes a long driveshaft (connected to the rear axle) to spin. There it meets a gear called a differential, which transfers the spinning motion so that the wheels roll forward or backward, and not sideways.

Front-wheel drive cars don't need a driveshaft because the axle is below the engine. But they still need a differential to turn the direction of the spinning 90 degrees.

Why It Works

Each piston moves up and down inside one of the engine's metal cylinders. First it moves down, to suck air and fuel into the cylinder. Then it's up again to squeeze that mixture. In the third step, the spark ignites the mixture, pushing the piston down. It moves up again in the last step, pushing exhaust out of the cylinder.

Spark plug

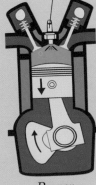

Induction   *Compression*   *Power*   *Exhaust*

All Kinds of Cars

Some cities, such as London and Paris, limit the traffic in the city centers by charging drivers an extra fee. The aim is to make traffic move more smoothly and to reduce pollution.

Economy Model

"Economy" means the savings in cost to buy—and to run— some cars. Most economy cars are small and light, so they don't need a powerful engine. A smaller engine needs to use less fuel, so the cost is less.

Things have changed a lot since the first few cars edged their way along city streets at the breathtaking speed of 5 miles per hour (8 kilometers per hour). Not only have cars become faster, but they have also become safer, more reliable, and more plentiful—with more than a billion in use around the world at last count.

Science is put to work all the time, helping engineers develop cars to cope with steep slopes, freezing temperatures, heavy loads . . . and wealthy drivers who demand luxury. Whether a driver wants to drive across the Sahara, commute to work or school comfortably, or deliver flowers to newlyweds, there's a car that suits that job best.

Luxury cars are engineered to provide a smooth ride and almost pure silence inside. Only the super wealthy can afford to buy the most expensive models, which can cost more than a house.

Jeeps

Jeeps were designed as army vehicles able to handle all sorts of roads—or sometimes no roads at all. Their suspension, steering, and tires make them well suited for rough terrain.

Modification

Amateur engineers and mechanics often turn their cars into more powerful or faster versions of the original cars. Modifying the engine, tires, and suspension of a family car can transform it into a racetrack competitor.

Can You Believe It?

Some cars have extra features that aren't scientific—or even necessary. People in the 1950s were fascinated by the first rockets being sent into space. American car designers decided to make cars look more like those rockets. They added enormous fins at the back to look like the fins on rockets. These had nothing to do with the cars' function, but people loved them.

11

Pickup Truck

Pickup trucks aren't much bigger than ordinary cars, but their powerful engines and larger storage capacity make them ideal for transporting goods. Many pickups have four-wheel drive to give them better traction and handling on rough or slippery terrain.

Keep on Trucking

The workhorses of the transportation world come in all shapes and sizes — each designed to carry out a job in the most scientific way possible. And for trucks, scientific means efficient and secure. Most trucks need large engines to push, pull, or carry heavy loads. Speed is less important than stability— balancing cargo or passengers safely and being able to steer and stop safely.

Precious load— steady as she goes!

Judging the center of mass is the important science behind the design of pickup trucks: The weight is balanced between the engine (front axle) and load (over the rear axle).

Packing a Load

Garbage and recycling trucks are equipped with compactors to let them carry up to six times the volume of uncompacted loads. With so much weight —including the compacting machinery—in the back, they need a third axle for support and grip.

School Bus Safety

Passenger safety is the most important engineering feature when designing and building school buses. Their great mass distributes the force of any collision. Seats are high, close together, and padded so that passengers are protected even if they aren't wearing seat belts.

Many school buses are equipped with routers so that children can connect to the Internet with Wi-Fi. It's ideal for getting a head start on homework if it's a long ride home.

13

First on the Scene

Emergency vehicles are there when you need them—they have to be. And they rely on a range of scientific and engineering features to do their job. Because emergencies call for urgent responses, these vehicles need to be fast. Police cars are often the most powerful versions of common vehicles such as SUVs and pickup trucks.

Other emergency vehicles resemble vans or trucks, but with special adaptations for their purpose such as medical treatment, firefighting, or mountain rescue. It is an engineering challenge to balance these special features with the need to get to and from emergency scenes quickly.

Ambulances are fitted with special noise filters so that the loud siren (needed to warn drivers and pedestrians) won't disturb patients inside the ambulance itself.

Ambulances

A whole range of engineering and electrical modifications help ambulances travel quickly and smoothly, while retaining contact with hospitals throughout. Special GPS equipment displays the fastest routes, often guiding ambulances up one-way streets in the wrong direction or on pedestrian-only streets.

14

Firefighting

Fire engines must be able to cope with house fires, brush fires, chemical fires, and blazes in city high-rises. Sometimes the team can't predict the type of fire until they arrive, so the truck must carry deluge guns and chemical tanks for electrical and chemical fires as well as the usual pumps, hoses, and ladders.

Mountain Rescue

Mountain rescue vehicles are specially adapted to cope with steep slopes, deep mud or water, snow, and ice . . . all while carrying a wide range of rescue and first-aid equipment. Injured hikers or skiers remain secure and stable even as the vehicle crosses the rockiest terrain.

Some city fire engines are equipped with ladders that can extend more than 131 feet (40 meters). The ladders are life savers if people are trapped inside rooms or if an outside fire escape has become unsafe.

Can You Believe It?

Weirdly, it seems that the noises made by the sirens on emergency vehicles are not very effective at alerting other drivers. Motorists only tend to notice the noises when the emergency vehicles are very near—and they may not notice at all if they're playing loud music! A recent study found that 90 percent of drivers' awareness of emergency vehicles was caused by the vehicles' flashing lights.

Henry Ford kept assembly lines rolling—and costs down—by telling customers that they could choose any color for their Fords, "as long as it's black."

The Assembly Line

America's Ford Motor Company began producing cars on assembly lines in 1913. A rope pulled a chassis along a straight assembly line, with 84 teams of workers, each concentrating on one task along the way. The new method reduced assembly time from 12 hours to 90 minutes. It revolutionized how factories —and not just car factories— could work more efficiently.

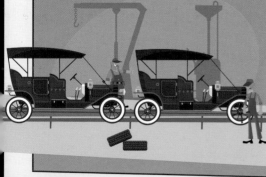

Roll Them Out!

The production of automobiles and trucks is one of the most important industries in the world. About 75 million new cars are produced worldwide each year. And just as cars themselves have developed over the years, so too have the ways that they're built. Engineering and technology advances have shaved time and cost from the manufacturing stage. A car, with its 1,800 parts, can now be built in less than a day.

Meanwhile, engineering and technology have both played a part in the testing process. No model can go into production until it has passed a series of tests—on computer screens, in labs, and on tracks outside.

Robots?

Nearly every modern car and truck is produced along an assembly line, but with one big difference compared to the 1913 Ford version. Human beings have been replaced by robots at many stages. Robots can work faster and more accurately than human workers, sometimes for 24 hours a day. China is now building a car factory that will be "all robot," with no human workers.

Many testing calculations work with the concept of torque, which is a measure of how much force acting on an object causes it to turn.

Test Driving

Each new car model is tested over and over again inside factories and on special tracks to measure a wide range of scientific, engineering, and safety aspects. Crash tests (with dummies replacing human passengers) measure the effects of impact at different speeds.

Try It Yourself

Pinpointing the center of mass is the key to many car-design tests. You can do your own test using a yardstick and a stone. Balance the stick on two extended fingers, then slide them together slowly—keeping the stick balanced—until they meet. That's the center of mass. Now try it again, but first have a friend balance a stone at one end of the stick. You'll find that the center of mass is much closer to the side with the stone.

Checkered Flag

Airplanes use airfoils on their wings to provide lift, but the upside-down airfoils on racing cars help do the opposite—stopping high-speed cars from flying off the road.

The Appliance of Science

Formula 1 manufacturers are constantly tinkering with their designs to get more speed. A typical car can accelerate from 0 to 62 miles per hour (100 kph) in two seconds. During that time it produces more g-forces than a spacecraft launch.

Ever since the first trucks and cars appeared on the scene, people have set up competitions to see which vehicle —or driver—is the fastest. And usually the winner is the one who has put science to use to cross the line first, or fastest.

Many Formula 1 engineering developments eventually find their way into family-car production. Tire design, aerodynamic (fuel-efficient) body shapes, and streamlined gearboxes have all become common.

I'm going to win—science is on my side!

Pure Speed

Drag racing is some of the fastest—and shortest—car racing around. It's all about acceleration. Some cars reach speeds of 335 miles per hour (540 kph) as they zoom down the 1,000 foot (305 m) track.

Ice-car racers in Canada and the United States use ordinary cars to race on frozen lakes. Drivers use the science of friction and Newton's Laws of Motion to prevent uncontrolled skids and crashes.

Demolition Derby

This crazy event isn't really a race— it's a competition to see which car can survive the most collisions. But some cars can be prepared either to "give" (absorb force safely) or to bounce away without much damage.

Ouch!

Try It Yourself

Fold an 8.5 x 11 inch (22 x 28 centimeter) sheet of paper so that the short sides meet in the middle. Fold them back and lay the paper on a table so that the folds turn the paper into a tunnel. Blow through along the tunnel and watch the paper roof get pushed down—just as a Formula 1 airfoil pushes the car down.

1

2

3

Brake lights shine more brightly than the vehicle's other lights to be highly visible in order to alert other drivers to slow down as well.

Controlling Speed

Truck and car designers try to improve the way vehicles can accelerate to help the drivers negotiate traffic and be able to maneuver quickly past obstacles. But it's just as important—if not more important—to be able to slow down quickly and safely.

Science plays a leading role in both of these aims. Car designers need to understand the basics about laws of motion in order to prevent dangerous accidents.

Brake Improvements

The Antilock Braking System (ABS) of most new cars senses when wheels will lock, allowing them to roll more slowly (with more steering control) rather than stopping. Brakes on older cars often locked on slippery surfaces, leading to dangerous skids.

Oh no, I'm skidding!

Sensing Danger

Brakes are linked to electronic systems that connect many parts of modern cars. Many new cars have electronic sensors that can detect when a pedestrian begins crossing the road—sending a signal to apply the brakes.

Sixty to Zero

Many cars are bought because they can move from a stop to 60 miles per hour (about 100 kph) super fast—even if drivers will rarely need to accelerate so quickly. But the real test is being able to design a car that can go from 60 to 0 quickly and safely, making roads much safer.

64 MPH

The hissing sound when a large truck slows down comes from its air brakes, a system that uses compressed air to apply extra force (friction) to slow the wheels' movement.

Fascinating Fact

"Stopping distance" is how far a car travels once the brakes have been applied. "Thinking distance" is how far the car goes before the driver reacts by braking. "Braking distance" is how much farther the car goes once the brakes have been hit. Stopping and braking distances increase with speed.

Thinking distance   *Braking distance*   *Stopped*

Unimog

One of the earliest all-terrain vehicles, the Unimog truck, trades off cargo capacity in favor of a flexible frame and high clearance off the ground.

Going Off-Road

For years, special trucks have been designed to go where cars couldn't—on rocky terrain, up steep slopes, or on snowy or muddy ground. Special tires, special climbing gears, and four-wheel drive provide traction.

Some of these features are now part of family cars called sports utility vehicles (SUVs). It's common for people to take these cars off-road into areas that were once too rugged for family cars. And engineering breakthroughs mean that cars might even double as boats or planes. The sky's the limit—or is it?

Some SUVs can climb slopes of 45 degrees—that means they're climbing the same distance that they're moving forward. The steepest street in the world measures only 19 degrees.

Submersible Cars

Cars designed to float—called car boats—have been around since the 1950s. Engineers have taken things a step further, or deeper. Once the driver of a Rinspeed sQuba floods the waterproof cockpit, the car sinks underwater and can travel like a submarine. The driver and passengers breathe through scuba-like tubes.

Four-Wheel Drive

The engines of most cars power movement in either the back axle (rear-wheel drive) or the front (front-wheel drive). Off-road vehicles have four-wheel drive, giving more secure traction on slippery or unstable surfaces. All-wheel drive (AWD) systems go further by sensing which wheels have a firmer grip—giving them more power and reducing power for wheels that aren't secure.

In some places, people call on four-wheel drive vehicles to drive students home if weather conditions suddenly become bad, making roads dangerous.

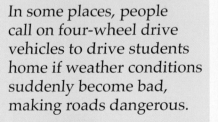

Can You Believe It?

The Lunar Roving Vehicle, or "moon buggy," was used on NASA's last three lunar missions in 1971 and 1972.

23

Monster Dump Trucks

The biggest construction jobs—building dams, digging mines, or blasting roads through mountains—call for the biggest, most powerful trucks on Earth. The largest uses an engine that packs about 4,000 horsepower!

Most family cars have engines of about 150 horsepower . . . dwarfed by comparison with monster trucks.

Some of the most dramatic vehicles on or off the road are genuine giants. Whether they're super long, super heavy, or super powerful, they harness science to make the best use of their scale.

Hand in hand with size is power. Yet again, Newton's Laws of Motion help explain why. Just as it takes more strength (force) to throw a bowling ball compared to a tennis ball, it takes a much larger engine to power these giants of the road than it does to power the engine of your much smaller family car.

Hey! It's my big brother!

Huge flatbed trucks carried 90 wind turbine blades (each more than 172 feet (52 m) long) up a 9,514-foot (2,900 m) mountain in China.

Stretch Limo

Engineers need to think big when they turn ordinary cars into eye-catching stretch limos. Several drivetrains are linked together to reach the rear axle, and electrical connectors ensure that power reaches the entire vehicle.

Moving House—Literally!

Special trucks are designed to carry enormous loads, including entire houses!

Multiple axles are needed to spread the enormous mass of the payload.

Can You Believe It?

Most big trucks have a tractor unit towing a large trailer. But the massive road trains of Australia have three or more trailers towed by a single tractor unit. The longest-ever road train had 112 trailers stretching 4,837 feet (1,474 m).

New Sources of Power

Electric Cars

Cars and trucks that run on electricity instead of gas or diesel produce hardly any air pollution. Their engines are almost silent. That cuts down on noise pollution, but creates the problem of how to warn pedestrians that a car is near them. There are plans to have these vehicles fitted with audible alert systems.

Truck and car exhaust is one of the worst contributors to global warming. It contains a gas called carbon dioxide, which collects in Earth's atmosphere and acts like a blanket, heating the planet.

Internal combustion engines have powered cars and trucks for well over a century, but the world now faces a problem—we might run out of fuel. The gasoline and diesel that make those engines run are produced from oil, and scientists can't agree on whether we will run out soon.

That's because oil is a fossil fuel, created over millions of years as plankton, or microscopic organisms, decay and become oil and natural gas. We're using up the fuel faster than it's being produced, so supplies aren't limitless. The race is on to build vehicles that will use less fossil fuels, or even use fuel that's produced from renewable sources.

NO FUEL!

Hybrid Vehicles

Some vehicles, called hybrids, use a mixture of gasoline and electric power. They have two motors. At low speeds, the electric motor powers the car. When more power is needed—to accelerate quickly or to climb—the gasoline motor takes over. But the electric motor also acts as a generator, storing electric power for when it's next needed.

Battery

Generator

Electric motor

Internal combustion engine

Power split device

The race is on to produce electric-car batteries that can be charged quickly and hold their charge for many hours. Charging stations, where people can recharge batteries, are becoming more common each year.

Hydrogen Alternative

Hydrogen is being tested as a nonpolluting alternative to fossil fuels, especially in heavy vehicles. Compressed hydrogen is converted to electricity to power the vehicle, and the only exhaust is water.

Fascinating Fact

There are different ways of calculating how fuel-efficient a vehicle is. For internal-combustion engines, the US, UK, and some other countries figure out how far (in miles) a gallon of gas will let a car travel (miles per gallon or mpg). Other countries use a system based on how many liters of gas are needed to travel 100 kilometers (L / 100 km).

It's not just trucks and cars that will be getting "smarter" in the future: Roads will also be linked to computer systems on trucks and cars. Information about road work, accidents, or unusual weather conditions will be fed into car systems.

The Future

Sometimes things that at first seem like problems can turn out to be inspiration for new inventions. For example, in recent decades, obstacles such as fossil fuels running out, overcrowding, and pollution have helped spark the development of electric vehicles and cleaner fuels.

With driverless cars already in production, the world is preparing for even more dramatic developments. Just as smartphones and the Internet keep people connected full time, vehicles will be constantly sending and receiving information to make driving safer and faster.

Flying Cars?

The idea of being able to hop into a car and then take off into the sky has been a fantasy for more than a century—but could it become a reality? The Terrafugia TF-X, still in the testing stage, is a flying car that can take off vertically and fly for up to 500 miles (800 km) at a cruising speed of 200 miles per hour (320 kph).

Kid's Eye View

A British company asked children to design cars for the future. Some kids left science out of the picture to concentrate on dragon-shaped vehicles and cupcake boosters to add power, but some other ideas could pave the way for real developments. Vehicle designers are already considering some of the ideas that came up, like color-changing materials and flexible glass for driving underwater.

Robot trucks will be able to carry passengers along fixed routes, like between airport terminals. Robot trucks are already carrying freight along highways in Arizona, stopping just before their destinations to let humans finish the drive.

"Calling All Cars"

Tiny cars—which take up hardly any space and can be summoned by smartphone —could help solve parking problems and provide low-cost transportation in the future.

Why It Works

A smartphone is really a computer as well as a communications device. And it combines the computing and communicating to figure out exactly where it is, using GPS (like the GPS in a car). When people call a mini-car, they're automatically telling the car where they are—so it can make its way to them.

Glossary

Aerodynamic Having a smooth, streamlined shape that reduces the effect of air resistance.

All-wheel drive An engine system (abbreviated as AWD) that provides power to wheels with good traction and reduces power to those with less traction.

Axle A shaft with turning wheels at each end.

Center of mass The point, sometimes called center of gravity, where all the mass of an object is concentrated.

Chassis The frame supporting the engine and body of a car or truck.

Collision An event in which two or more objects come together and then change direction.

Compressed air Air that has been pumped into a container, and which is released with great force.

Crankshaft A long metal rod that helps the engine turn the wheels of a vehicle.

Cylinder A chamber housing a piston in an internal combustion engine.

Deluge gun A high-powered, aimable water jet that is used in firefighting.

Differential A rotating, angled gear that changes the direction of rotation.

Drivetrain The system that connects a motor vehicle's engine with the drive axle.

Energy The ability to do work.

Exhaust The waste gas given off by an engine during internal combustion.

Force The push or pull on an object when it meets another object.

Fossil fuel A fuel, such as oil, coal, or natural gas that is produced over millions of years from the remains of living things.

Four-wheel drive An engine system that provides power to the front and rear axles, so that all four wheels are powered.

Friction The resistance of something to motion, often causing a moving object to slow down.

Fuel-efficient Able to produce power using relatively little fuel.

G-force A measure of force on an object, representing the amount of force that gravity has on that object.

Gearbox A set of gears, inside a casing, that provides the most efficient way of transferring energy from the engine to the wheels.

Global warming An overall increase in world temperature caused by a combination of natural actions, such as volcanic eruptions, and human-made effects, such as gases produced by powered vehicles.

GPS An abbreviation of Global Positioning System, a method of locating a position on Earth by communicating with satellites.

Impact The meeting of objects with great force.

Industrial Revolution A period in the eighteenth and nineteenth centuries when inventors and engineers developed new machines using steam and other sources of power.

Internal combustion A system of providing power by burning a mixture of gasoline (or other burnable fuel) and air inside an engine; the hot gases produced expand and drive pistons.

Mass The amount of matter in an object.

Newton's Laws of Motion A set of three basic laws, proposed by English scientist Isaac Newton, to describe how an object reacts to forces acting on it.

Torque The ability of a force to produce a twisting motion.

Index